TBOX ON TEST: Direct Rail Services supplied celebrity split-headcode Class 37/0 No. 37087 *Keighley & Worth Valley Railway* to ide power for a series of test runs in mid-March designed to evaluate upgrades to New Measurement Train vehicles Nos. 977984 7993. On the 11th, the 'Tractor' was recorded at Streetly Gate in the West Midlands working a circular 1Q69 10.55 Derby to y, the two Mk. 3s being sandwiched by ex-Gatwick Express Mk. 2s Nos. 72616 & 72639 in use as barriers/brake force runners. BSO was provided, so the diagram required No. 37087 to run round its train several times. Simon Ede

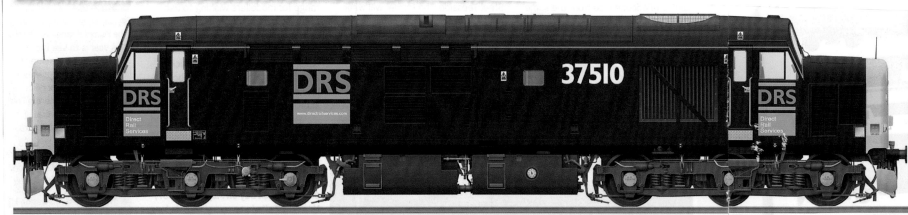

● Class 37/5 No. 37510 in Direct Rail Services Oxford blue livery with miniature snowploughs

● Class 37/5 No. 37688 *Kingmoor TMD* in Direct Rail Services Oxford blue livery with miniature snowploughs

DRS - The Early Years

The story of Direct Rail Services is a remarkable one by any standards. It is a company which started out with no locomotives and worse than that, no trains to haul! They didn't have a depot, just a few rusty sidings at a nuclear plant in a remote and difficult to access part of the Cumbrian coast. Even when they got some locomotives, they had nowhere to fuel them and a road tanker had to be hired-in! In reality, they should have lasted five minutes but the chance to buy a handful of Class 20s which had been used in the construction of the Channel Tunnel in 1994 got the wheels turning. Competing against long-established companies like EWS and Freightliner was never going to be easy but as time moved on, the hard work paid off and from West Coast Class 66-hauled Intermodals to Class 20s on the flask and water cannon trains and a well equipped maintenance depot at Carlisle Kingmoor, today the company is at the top of its game.

With the purchase of former British Rail Class 20, 33, 37 and 47 locomotives, DRS has always been popular with enthusiasts and while just about every other train company in the UK has dispensed with these traditional British built locomotives, DRS continue to purchase, operate, maintain and refurbish them. The fact they chose an attractive blue livery also helped.

The aim of this book is to look at the locomotives and trains operated by DRS in their early years. What you call the 'early years' is open to interpretation so what I've done is to concentrate on 1994 to 2005, a period when Classes 08, 20/9, 33 and 87 were in use alongside the 20/3s, 37s and 47s. If you like, this is basically the book featuring all locos which were painted into the original DRS livery. I've looked briefly at the Class 57s and 66s but these will feature fully in a second volume. This is not a history book by any means and not every major event is included.

I would like to extend a massive thank you to Gordon Ogden, whose images have been used throughout. With the exception of just four, this is all his work. I'd like to thank Keith Hayton for his images, David Umpleby for laying out the book, his research and attention to detail, Jason Prescott for the superb graphics and making it all come to life, Julie Ryan for the scanning and my wife Mary for her constant support and help with the text.

Enjoy the book
Nick Meskell
February 2011

Front cover: Class 20/9 locomotives on the S&C just north of Blea Moor on 27th June 1999 with 20906+20904 and a driver training/route learning run from Carlisle back to Carlisle via Preston and Blackburn.

DRS - A Brief History

In 1995, as the privatisation of British Rail was almost completed, a company was launched by British Nuclear Fuels for the purpose of taking over the operation of trains from the various rail connected power stations in the UK and running them to the plant at Sellafield. Known as Direct Rail Services, starting a new company was no mean task as at that time you simply couldn't 'buy' a locomotive! The glut of surplus and withdrawn locomotives which litter the sidings country-wide today didn't exist back in the mid-1990s. Classes such as 33, 37, 47, 56 and 58 were still used daily, the Class 66 was many years off and although various locomotives were withdrawn or stored as such, they were often overdue overhauls, accident damaged or heavily robbed for spares so the process of buying one, refurbishing and operating it yourself was extremely costly and almost impossible.

With relatively light trains to haul, the company did not need powerful locos and speed wasn't such an issue either so the Class 20 was an ideal choice. As luck would have it, various locos that were used in the construction of the Channel Tunnel had become available. These were mostly ex-BR Class 20/0 locomotives, some were privately owned, and in total, 24 of them had been used. Painted in their RFS livery and renumbered 2001 upwards, once back in the UK in 1993, these locos were simply stored and DRS purchased most of them. Five duly received an extensive overhaul at Brush in Loughborough. The first completed loco moved to the Great Central Railway for testing in September 1995 and the 20/3 sub-class that we know today was born. DRS was in the haulage business.

With essentially two pairs of locomotives (normally coupled nose-to-nose) and a spare the new 20/3s didn't have a great deal of work. Most of this involved short out and back workings on the Cumbrian coast from Sellafield to Barrow and Drigg. The movement of nuclear flasks around the UK was still in the hands of what had become Transrail and for example, in 1995/96 there were a handful of Class 31/1s in the LWNC pool based at Wigan Springs Branch which were often used in pairs to and from Sellafield.

From February 1996, with the merger of Transrail, Loadhaul, Mainline and Rail Express Systems under the new EWS banner, a huge surplus of locomotives was created. With 250 brand new Class 66s looming, a mixed bag of locos from 08s to 47s were put up for sale and duly purchased by DRS. It's beyond the scope of this book to list everything which was bought – and there doesn't appear to be a comprehensive and accurate list anyway – it was never the intention to refurbish and operate all of them. Many were life expired and beyond repair, others were bought specifically for spares but nevertheless, some fine machines were acquired over the years, such as 37012 'Loch Rannoch' and 47484 'Isambard Kingdom Brunel'. Sadly, neither of these two made it back.

Around the time the first Class 66s were arriving on our shores there was trouble with the Nightstar project. Conceived in 1992 and progressing slowly until 1997, Nightstar was a proposed overnight sleeper service from Amsterdam, Dortmund and Frankfurt via the Channel Tunnel to Glasgow, London, Manchester, Plymouth and Swansea. Class 92s were to haul the trains over the electrified sections with pairs of 37/6s at either end of generator coach to work to Plymouth and Swansea. In total, twelve Class

---

With trainloads as small as this the Class 20 was the perfect locomotive for the early years. This Class 20/9 and 20/3 combination pictured at Leeds was not that common as they could not work in multiple.

From the Southern Region to Cumbria, the Class 33 locomotives were an interesting purchase, in particular the narrow bodied 33/2s. Four Class 33s have been operated by DRS.

37/5s were refurbished at Doncaster Works in 1995/1996, emerging as 37601 to 37612. Regarded as surplus and used occasionally to haul out-of-service Eurostar sets, the failure of Nightstar was of great benefit to DRS which purchased 37607 to 37612 in July 1997. Eventually all twelve moved to DRS ownership.

As well as the regular flask and acid trains, the company started to pick up other work. Demand was always high for railtour duties and diesel galas. More commercial opportunities came in the shape of the 'minimodal' Intermodal trials, a milk train and even haulage of the Royal train. A major flow, commencing in 2001, was the start of regular DRS powered overnight Intermodal trains between Grangemouth and Daventry. Known as the 'Malcolm' trains, Preston station was the place to be circa midnight when a pair of 37s in each direction, literally minutes apart, shattered the silence! This was a turning point for the company as from humble beginnings, DRS was now working alongside Freightliner and EWS on the high profile and money-making West Coast Main Line container business.

As work increased, with it came more locomotives. Ten more Class 20s were on stream by the end of 1998, numbered 20306 to 20315. Used mainly for the mundane flask trains, these ten were made of eight former BR/EWS 20/0s and two more which had been used in the Channel Tunnel. Various other ex-RFS locos were considered at the time, but locos such as 20075 in its British Rail Telecoms green and grey livery were in better condition.

Another major purchase in August 1998 was all six 20/9s. Owned by Hunslet Barclay and used for weed killing duties, this is often seen as a strange twist in the DRS story. Although bought for spares, they were actually in a good enough condition to operate and so they did, all except 20905. As these were unrefurbished locos, simply ex-BR 20/0s, they were incompatible with the 20/3s. In addition, just how many Class 20s were needed? Fifteen 20/3s equated to seven pairs plus a spare and given the fact they could not work Intermodals or any high speed/high profile services, was there ever a need for so many? At one point it would seem DRS had bought or considered just about ever Type 1 in existence and

The Class 37 has become the largest class of ex-BR locomotive to run for DRS. In ex-works condition, this is 37259 a former EWS machine now used to haul trains once worked by EWS Class 37s.

even 20209 which was originally to be converted to 20907 was included in the purchase from Hunslet Barclay. Eventually the 20/9s were sold off. Of the many other locomotives purchased over the years, inroads were made towards overhauling and returning a number of them to service whilst others were stripped and scrapped. The company decided on Classes 33, 37 and 47 and over a period of years, various locos passed through the works at Doncaster, Glasgow and Loughborough. Depending on the level of work required, some engines seemed to take literally years from start to finish whereas others were far quicker. For the Class 37/0s in particular, some emerged with fully enclosed/sealed nose ends and modern head/tail light clusters whereas others, such as 37029 and 37087 came on line with their split headcode boxes, traditional marker lights and the BR-fitted single headlight of the late 1980s.

Of the Class 33s purchased, four made it into service, three 33/0s and one 33/2. Of the many Class 47s purchased, four also made it, two 47/0s and two 47/4s. By the early 2000s, with the ETS fitted 33s and 47s, DRS locos could now provide train supply, allowing for use on passenger trains. The

The company started out with just the four operational Class 47s but that has increased in recent years. The simple DRS livery suited these locomotives well.

operation of 47s also meant the company had locos with a maximum speed of 95mph for the first time. Useless for flask trains, 95mph meant they could be pathed alongside other express passenger trains and they could also be hired to the likes of Virgin Trains for their Cross Country and West Coast diesel operations as well as The West Coast Railway Company for charter duties.

By 2003 the company had a considerable number of operational locomotives including twenty Class 20s and sixteen Class 37s. As well as the withdrawn/stored locos purchased directly from EWS, a number were acquired from Ian Riley Engineering, based on the East Lancs Railway at Bury and the Harry Needle Railroad Company at Barrow Hill. These were mainly operational or at least 'intact' and had been used, albeit on a limited basis, by both companies. Various levels of work were required to bring them up to DRS standards, for some just a repaint, for others more extensive. The acquisition of these locos added a bit of fizz to the DRS Class 37 story whereas the 37/6s were almost mint ex-works, while some of the 37/0s retained original fittings and features.

The Class 20/9s used to work on weed killing trains until they were bought by DRS in 1998. After six years of ownership all six were resold. This red stripe livery was unique to these locos.

From time to time DRS have hired in locos from other companies and in 2006 when they tied up a short term deal with Riviera Trains this large logo livered Type 4 was moved to Kingmoor.

As good as these 37s and 47s were, in order to compete with the likes of Freightliner and EWS for more freight work the company turned to the Class 66. In October and November 2003, ten of these brand new machines were offloaded at Newport docks and the Class 66/4 was born. Taking over from the pairs of 37s (or 47s) on Intermodal services, the introduction of these locos took the DRS story in another direction. In later years, the purchase and refurbishment of 37s, 47s and latterly 57s continued but when 66401 and friends came on line, many of the locos purchased and earmarked for a return were sold off or scrapped. As previously mentioned, what fun we could have had with ex-Scottish celebrities 37012 'Loch Rannoch' and 37043 'Loch Lomond'. Both locos were at Loughborough in 2002, although to be fair they were probably only ever going to be stripped for spares. There is no doubt the year 2003 was a turning point.

Trials with Class 87s in 2004 came to nothing, the four Class 33s went to the West Coast Railway Company (in exchange for two Class 37s) and by 2008 the company had 34 Class 66s on its books. Seriously overpowered

for use on flask or water cannon trains, at one point it looked as if DRS was contemplating a switch to complete Class 66 operation, as per the other three major freight companies, and overhauls to 37s and 47s decreased or never commenced.

A further twist came in 2008/2009 when the company returned 66401 to 66410 back to the leasing company and the overhauls of 37s and 47s recommenced along with the purchase of nine former Freightliner Class 57/0s.

Away from the operation of trains, the company as such has always seemed to maintain a friendly and pro-active face. Maintaining traditional railway practices, such as naming their locomotives and holding regular depot open days has won DRS many friends, while the fact they have a fleet of interesting and traditional locomotives is merely coincidental. However, make no mistake about it, the 37s and 47s are very popular, as too are the stylish blue liveries they carry, and that's probably why many railway enthusiasts have an interest in DRS and its locomotives!

The leasing of Class 66 locomotives from 2003 took the company in a different direction and it was able to compete with the two big freight hauliers for lucrative contracts.

CLASS 20

Class 20 Locomotives: 1994 to 2006					
DRS Number	BR Number	CT Number	Purchased	DRS Livery	Sold
20301	20047	2004	10/94	09/95	
20302	20084	2002	10/94	10/95	
20303	20127	2018	10/94	10/95	
20304	20120	2009	10/94	10/95	
20305	20095	2020	10/94	11/95	
20306	20131		07/97	02/98	
20307	20128		07/97	02/98	
20308	20187		07/97	03/98	
20309	20075		07/97	03/98	
20310	20190		07/97	03/98	
20311	20102	2008	10/94	03/98	
20312	20042		09/97	09/98	
20313	20194	2006	09/97	10/98	
20314	20117		07/97	11/98	
20315	20104		07/97	12/98	
20901	(20101)		08/98	09/99	11/04
20902	(20060)		08/98	08/99	06/04
20903	(20083)		08/98	08/99	11/04
20904	(20041)		08/98	04/00	11/04
20905	(20225)		08/98	05/03	11/04
20906	(20219)		08/98	11/99	11/04

The 20/9s had already been renumbered in that series prior to being purchased by DRS. The previous BR numbers are shown for completeness. 20901 and 20904 only ever carried the DRS red stripe livery; 20902, 20903 and 20906 carried both the red stripe livery and the standard blue livery; 20905 only ever carried the standard blue livery. They were all sold to HNRC.

Locomotives Named
20301 'Furness Railway 150' - Workington Station, 1st June 1996 (Removed January 2000)
20301 'Max Joule 1958-1999' - Kingmoor depot, 4th February 2000

Page 7 top: With their role on the Channel Tunnel construction complete, the 24 Class 20 locomotives returned to the UK in 1993. All except the privately owned ones were essentially dumped here at Doncaster. Although in good condition, the Class 20 was certainly out of favour at this time. The remaining serviceable BR-owned locos were stored or withdrawn during 1993 and by January 1994, just a couple were active, alongside the eleven British Rail Telecoms 20/0s (even some of these were stored) and the six Hunslet Barclay 20/9s. Had DRS (or British Nuclear Fuels as they were still known in 1994) not required some engines, they would probably all have been scrapped. In the end, DRS purchased 15 of the 24 repatriated locos including this motley looking bunch at Doncaster, headed by 2010 (20159).

Right: In the end, of the 15 purchased, remarkably only seven ever made it as 20/3s. The rest were systematically stripped and moved to various locations over the years. One of the unlucky candidates was this machine, 2007, TOPS number 20175. Overhauled in February 1992, shipped to France in March of the same year and back home in August 1993, the loco was moved to Doncaster on 1st September 1993. Purchased by DRS thirteen months later, the loco was moved to Sellafield, Brush Works in Loughborough and finally to Kingmoor in December 1999 where it was scrapped four years later. Completely stripped at this time, this image shows the loco at Loughborough. Of thc six ex-Tunnel locos that made it as 20/3s, it is often wondered how 'good' or 'bad' the other nine were. Having had the asbestos removed at Glasgow Works in 1992 and described as 'overhauled' did it really take fifteen locos to make six good ones?

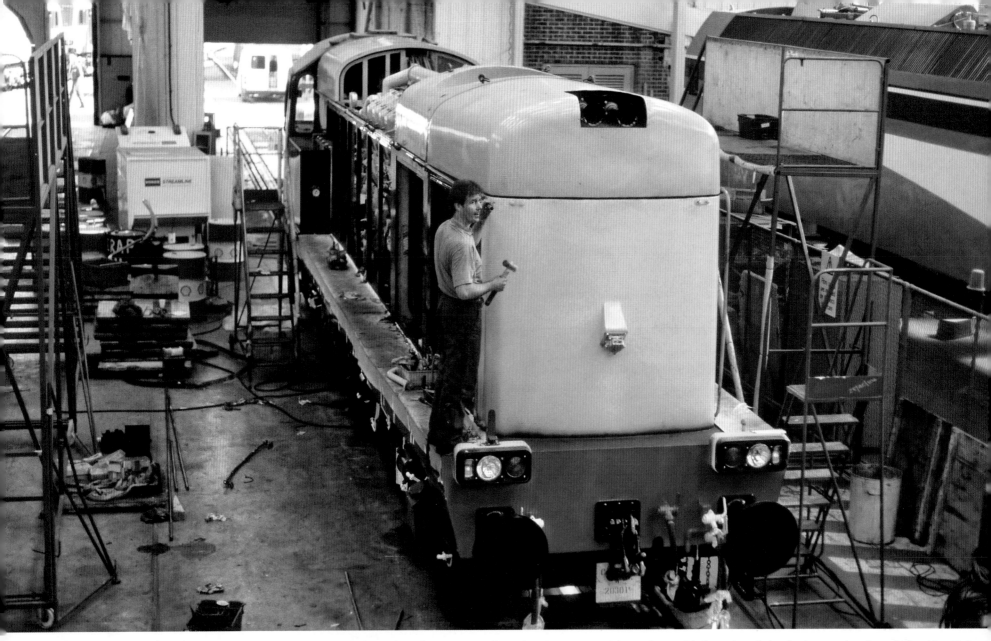

Brush Works in Loughborough in June 1995 with 20047 (2004) in the process of overhaul. At this stage the new flat fronted nose-end look of the locomotive was visible. With all trace of the disc indicators and red and white marker lights removed, two group standard headlight clusters and the multiple working socket were in place. On the buffer beam, the former blue star multi-working cables, vacuum brake pipe and, if it had one, through steam heat pipe were removed leaving a very tidy surface with just the air brake hoses, hook and shackle. Note the yellow end which, at the time of this photo, did not extend all the way to the roof. Of interest, whilst these humble Type 1s were going through a rework, thirteen state-of-the-art Class 9/1 'Eurotunnel' locos were under construction, as seen to the right.

Left: This is 20302 (ex-2002/20084) in the earlier stages of its overhaul with a third loco, presumably 20303 (ex-2018/20127) behind. Upon completion these locos were often described as 'new' or 'better than when new' and when you see the level of work that was undertaken this may well have been true. Raised on trestles, the loco really has been stripped bare. The last time it would have looked like this would have been sometime in 1961 at the RSH Workshops in Darlington! Probably irrelevant but note that the locos are positioned nose to nose. When you see classic workshop photos from years gone by, the locos were always the same way around to allow the fitting of components etc in the No.1 end/No.2 end etc.

Right: DRS struck a deal with the Great Central Railway to test their 'new' 20/3s and 20301 was moved to Quorn on 21st September 1995. Seven days later the tests were deemed successful and the loco moved by road to Sellafield. 20302 to 20304 followed a similar pattern and were all at Sellafield by Christmas 1995. The final loco, 20305, went straight to Sellafield untested, was duly stored, moved to the Great Central in June 1996 and then back to Sellafield later that month. This image shows 20305 upon arrival at Sellafield first time around in December 1995. Note the lack of DRS branding.

As recorded previously, although the 20/3s came on stream in 1995, it was 1999 before the company took over the complete operation of nuclear trains. In the interim years, DRS locomotives undertook a mixed bag of duties, one of the most high profile was haulage of the Royal Train by 20301 and 20302 from Crewe to Aberystwyth on 30th/31st May 1996. Prior to the working, both locos had to demonstrate their haulage and braking capabilities and ran from Crewe to Holyhead and back. This photo shows 20302 at Holyhead, coupled to a rake of Royal Mail/RES liveried BG and GUV coaches. 20301 was also present but not shown here.

Top: There's a great deal of irony attached to the fact that one day these Class 20s are hauling flask and acid trains - probably the least glamorous freight flows on the network – and then the next day, here they are atop the Royal train – probably the most attractive and luxurious train on the network! This is Machynlleth on 30th May 1996 with 20301 leading. The train had started out from Wolverhampton during the afternoon and stabled here overnight with the Royal party, including HM The Queen, still on board. The train crew were also allowed on board and given private compartments! Early the following morning the train continued the 20.5 miles to Aberystwyth and after the Royal party had alighted, returned empty stock to Crewe. During the course of this two day adventure, 20303 was on standby at Crewe. Of course, the reason the Class 20s were required for this journey was because of their 'go-almost-anywhere' route availability of 5. At this time in 1996, the Royal Train was usually hauled by 47798 'Prince William' and 47799 'Prince Henry' but with these 47/4s having an RA6 rating, they could not be used. Note the spotless silver buffers on 20301. As it stands, this may well have been the last time the Royal Train was hauled by locomotives that were owned by a British company. From 1996, the American-owned EWS provided the power, from 2001, the Canadian National Railway purchased EWS, duly taking over the operation and from June 2007, it has been undertaken by the Berlin-based German National Railway company Deutsche Bahn AG, under the UK banner of DB Schenker.

Bottom: Guess the location? In the early days of DRS operations the Class 20s were often used to keep driver route knowledge up to date which saw them visit many DMU-only branch lines. This is Largs station in south west Scotland, usually an EMU-only terminus destination, with 20302 and 20303 in 1997. With Hunterston Power Station some five miles further south, flask trains would not normally have to come this far but route knowledge was still maintained in case of failure and/or emergency working.

20302, 20301 and 20303 head an impressive rake of nine Inter City liveried Mark 1 coaches at Workington on 1st June 1996. This was a landmark day in the history of the company as not only was this the first charter train powered by Class 20/3s, the first naming ceremony of the class took place when Max Joule, the Managing Director of DRS named 20301 'Furness Railway 150'. The small circular plaque is just about visible on the second loco although, go back a page and it can be seen at Machynlleth the previous day! The tour itself was of interest, operated by Pathfinder and named The Cumbrian Coaster it started out at 05.50 from Bristol Temple Meads with the Eurostar-owned 37604+37611 in charge. (Two locos that would, of course end up in DRS ownership in later years). At Crewe, 20302+20301/20303 (fresh from Royal duty) took over. It is often forgotten that initially the 20/3s did not have the multi-working sockets on their cab ends so a triple header as such was not possible and on this occasion, 20303 was just dead-in-tow. At Carnforth an extra driver was provided for 20303 which was duly started and provided a double/single tandem journey through to Workington. After a one hour 40 minute layover, the trio worked back south as far as Sellafield. Here, 20303 was taken off, leaving 20301+20302 to work back to Carnforth and then 37611+37604 resumed control and blazed back to Bristol, arriving just before 23.00.

Top: For four weeks in July 1997, DRS ran trial milk trains from Penrith to Cricklewood. The train only ever operated with one loaded vehicle with a couple of flats to provide brake force and it was allowed to travel at 75mph, becoming the first DRS train permitted to travel at this speed. On the outward journey, the train usually recessed in the Up Sidings at Nuneaton to await the arrival of a conductor for the driver. In this image, 20303+20304 pose nicely for the camera. Note the miniature snowploughs and 'MILKLINER 2000' sticker on 20303. Departure from Penrith was late afternoon with the train finally arriving at Cricklewood circa 22.00. Here the locos detached and ran to St. Pancras for stabling. Some 24 hours later, they returned light to Cricklewood and worked back to Cumbria. One of the little known facts about this train is that it never carried any milk! The trial was simply to see if a container/train was a viable way of moving the white stuff and although the train was successful, it did what it had to do and 10, 12, 15 or more tanks of milk could have been conveyed the option to move milk by rail was never pursued. (Perhaps the cows moved instead?).

Bottom: Tank Freight meets Eurostar! Towards the end of the trial, DRS had just acquired the first of their 37/6s and these too were given a trial on this train. This is Penrith with 20303 next to 37609+37610. Complete with a proper 'MILKLINER 2000' headboard affixed to the offside lamp bracket, note that 37609 has had its Eurostar 'rings' removed and in their place a rather crude 'TF' logo and the words 'Tank Freight' underneath. Although a pair of locomotives was an operating requirement for flask trains, what a terrible waste of fuel and power a pair of 37s is to haul one (empty) wagon and a few flats.

Above: This delightful shot taken at Park South Junction shows 20301+20302 on 12th May 1999, working a single KYA wagon from Sellafield into the docks at Barrow.

Right: This is another historic working with 20304 and a sister loco on what was the first booked train for DRS power. It is often forgotten that when DRS was conceived it didn't actually have any regular work. Although BNFL operated trains and intended to use their own locomotives at some point, their trains were contracted to Transrail/EWS. This particular flow was for Kemira, a chemicals company based in Helsinki, Finland and it ran twice a week. The train itself took loaded acid tanks from the Kemira plant at Helsby to Sellafield. This 1996 shot was taken at West Cheshire Junction.

Left: The second naming ceremony to involve a DRS locomotive came about through unhappy circumstances following the death of Max Joule, the Managing Director of the company. Described as 'the driving force' behind DRS, Mr Joule was tragically killed in an accident in 1999. To mark his passing, 20301 was de-named in early 2000, given a heavy clean and polish and a single nameplate was affixed on the cab end. The name was unveiled in a private family ceremony at Kingmoor depot on 4th February 2000 and the name is still carried today. The photo shows 20301 just after the naming ceremony.

Right: Although not actually part of the 20/3 story, this image is included to show what could have happened regarding 20094. Pictured here in the company of 20301 at Kingmoor, the loco was initially preserved and the important job of removing the asbestos was carried out in 1994. Moved around, the loco ended up at Barrow Hill in 1999 and was sold to DRS in December 2000, moving to Kingmoor a year later. A detailed restoration/overhaul had already commenced, as can be seen, but the loco was instead taken to Glasgow Works to be stripped for spares. This never took place and it was moved to the Churnet Valley Railway in 2004 where it was finally stripped and scrapped.

Two years down the line, it was the summer of 1997 when the second phase of major locomotives purchase took place. Six 37/6s, some of which had been previously leased to the company (see Class 37 section) were purchased outright in July 1997 and that summer also saw a further spending spree with the acquisition of just about every Class 20 left on the UK rail network. These included the last four serviceable Class 20/0s, - 075, 128, 131 and 187 - now owned by Racal-BRT and working off Bescot, allocated to the TAKB pool. Various other ex-BRT 20s in the TAKX (stored) pool were acquired and collected from the depots at Crewe and Bescot. An unusual purchase was that of 20042, owned by Pete

Waterman and painted in the all black Waterman livery. This particular locomotive had appeared at various diesel galas, (notably the ELR Gala in 1996), paired with its matching sister 20188 and they were often the star attraction. Taking into account the ex-Channel Tunnel locomotives purchased back in 1994 but not used in the first batch of overhauls and the 1997 acquisitions, a further ten locos were selected to become 20306 to 20315 and overhauls commenced at Doncaster with 20131. This image shows 20075 and another ex-BRT liveried loco at Carnforth on their way to Doncaster for overhaul.

Left: Two images of 20307 – before and after. Eight of the former BRT-owned 20/0s were considered good enough and made it to Doncaster for overhaul to 20/3s. This is 20128 at Doncaster with 20131 latterly 20306 behind. This loco emerged in March 1998.

Right: The completed job. A delightful image of a gorgeous work stained 20307 on Kingmoor depot. This is a good opportunity to compare the nose end detail of a 20/0 to the second batch of 20/3s. Note the large high level headlight. It is believed these 20/3s were the first UK locomotives to be fitted with this kind of light, thus giving the triangle effect of white lights seen today.

Above: Two shots from 2001 showing the Class 20/3s on their normal duties at this time. This is Bridgwater in Somerset, near to Hinkley Point Power Station, with 20315+20313 loading/unloading flasks on to the FNA wagons. The location here is a stub of the old docks branch line, closed in 1967, almost adjacent to Bridgwater Station (still open). Note the cab end multi-working socket which was fitted to all the second batch of 20/3s upon rebuild in 1998 and subsequently fitted to all of the first batch. This train runs to/from Crewe.

Right: Another out and back run involving much less mileage is from Crewe to Valley in North Wales, serving the Wylfa Nuclear Power Station. In this shot 20311+20315 pause with their train under the loading facility on 23rd May 2002. Originally the maximum speed a flask train could travel at was 45mph. This was latterly revised to 60mph when empty and 45 when loaded and then revised again to 60mph for both.

A more recent shot of a spotless 20311+20315 near to Teeside Airport on 6th August 2007 with the 4Z44 working from Haverton Hill to Kingmoor. This out and back flow takes the Megafret flats for maintenance. In this image, 20311 carries the name 'Class 20 'Fifty''. This was applied at the DRS open day at Kingmoor on 7th July 2007.

The third and final major acquisition of Class 20s involved the purchase of the 20/9s from Hunslet Barclay. This took place in August 1998, when the overhaul to the second batch of 20/3s was about half complete. It was widely reported that these locos had been bought solely for spares but latterly discovered that they were in fact in a good enough condition to use in service without requiring much attention. All six were named and all retained their disc headcodes except for 20905 and 20906 which had the centre box design. This photo shows the typical consist of the weed killing train of the 1990s with various coaches and tanks sandwiched between the locomotives. The train itself was through fitted so both locos took power at the same time. This is the Warehouse Yard at Carlisle Upperby with 20903 'Alison' and 20901 'Nancy'.

Left: 20905, de-named, but still with the Hunslet Barclay branding and livery at the north end of Kingmoor shed in early 1999. By the end of 1998 five of the six 20/9s had been whisked off to Crewe for repaints leaving 20905 as the sole survivor in this livery for many years. Receiving an overhaul at Doncaster in early 2003, it was displayed at the Open Weekend at Doncaster in July 2003, fully restored and repainted into the normal DRS livery. Moving to Kingmoor it was just assumed it would be used but it never was, although it pottered around the depot, moving other locos and wagons. Almost 18 months after its overhaul the loco was sold to the Harry Needle Railroad Company (HNRC) where it was repainted into Railfreight Unbranded livery and has become one of their most used Class 20s. Why this locomotive was so much out of favour with DRS will never be known, particularly as it had been overhauled and repainted to such a high standard.

Right: One of the lesser known and least photographed trains operated by DRS is the short out and back run from Sellafield to Drigg. With a distance of about four miles in each direction, the trains usually consist of just a few wagons and can run once a day and then not at all for weeks. As the flow is such a short working it can easily be pathed between the DMUs but of more interest, it utilises any loco stabled at Sellafield. For a short while in 1998/1999, 08375 was hired and used on these trains. The journey shown here just out of Sellafield from July 1999 features 20902 de-named but still Hunslet-Barclay branded. Running nose first, the train would require two drivers, one of whom would be a trainman, in charge of marshalling and preparing the train.

Left: 20902+20903 in Hunslet Barclay two tone grey but with the branding and 'Lorna'/'Alison' nameplates removed.

Judging by the external condition of these two locos you'd presume they'd been repainted and the second one has received a new set of bogies! This was not the case as both 20902+20903 had been de-named, de-vinyled and given a heavy clean and touch up. This had to be done at some point anyway so why not do it in time for the Keighley and Worth Valley Railway gala, held over the weekend of 31st July/1st August 1999. The previous year, DRS had sent 20308+20311. This time around they supplied four locos, the two 20s plus 37612 (in DRS livery) and 37604 (in EPS livery and on loan at the time).

Left: This is Hellifield with 20s topping the 37s and a rake of Mark 1s on their way to the event. The coaches were an air braked set from the WCRC, thus allowing the 20s to work them.

Top right: The bizarre sight of a Class 20/9 nose first at Keighley Station.

Bottom right: Oxenhope on the Sunday morning of the event with the 20s started up and ready for action.

Left: With fifteen Class 20/3s making seven pairs and a spare engine and the five 20/9s (discounting 20905) making two more pairs plus a spare, you'd imagine that, on paper at least, nine pairs of locomotives was sufficient and would meet traffic demands. Well, just like the England football team which looks great on paper but is hopeless on grass, it didn't work out and the pairing of 20/9s and 20/3s took place quite often. The image opposite shows 20902 with 20309 at Dent hauling a flask wagon back to Carlisle following maintenance at Doncaster. The biggest problem here, of course, is that the locomotives cannot work in multiple and this was thought to be the main reason why the 20/9s fell out of favour as quickly as they did. Still retaining the BR fitted blue star multiple working, the 20/9s could work with many classes including 31s, 33s and 37s and other Class 20/0s and 20/9s, but they were completely incompatible with the 20/3s and their in-house system. On trains like the one shown opposite left it probably didn't matter. After all with just the one flask, a dead 20/3 at 73 tonnes was not a problem but when it came to changing ends, re-marshalling trains or shunting, the locos had to be started up/shut down separately, the cabs were different (the 20/9s had FOUR seats!) and numerous other unwanted factors came into play.

Below: 20904 pictured in May 2000 at the north end of Kingmoor yard basking in the sun after its recent repaint at LNWR, Crewe. As recorded previously, five of the 20/9s were dispatched for DRS house colours within a year of purchase and 901, 902, 903 and 906 were all completed by the end of 1999. 20904 duly became the last working member of the class to run in Hunslet-Barclay livery and this was repainted in April 2000. As can be seen in this image and subsequent pages, these five locos unusually retained the red stripe on their solebar. In later years, 20902, 20903, 20905 and 20906 received the 'normal' DRS livery, minus the red solebar but for 20901 and the featured loco, 20904, this was its one and only repaint prior to its subsequent sale in 2004.

Coupled together, with their blue star multi-working and smart DRS colours, by the early 2000s the 20/9s started to work far and wide on flask trains and other duties. This lovely image shows 20904 and 20906 at Clydeport in North Ayrshire, the crane terminal for Hunterston Power Station. The train here was 7S52 from Kingmoor. Note the slight variation in the DRS branding and please, don't mention the colour of their roofs! There doesn't appear to be a common colour used at any particular time and on any particular batch. Roof colours are invariably grey, light blue, normal blue or even black!

Left: 20903+20901 pause at Monktonhall Junction working 7S43, the 03.06 from Kingmoor to Torness. Behind the locos are two empty flat wagons which were used as barriers at either end of the FNA wagons at this time. Torness Nuclear Power Station is situated near Dunbar, East Lothian, in eastern Scotland, just a few miles south of the Oxwellmains Cement Works on the East Coast Main Line. The Power Station itself was the last of the second generation of power plants to be commissioned in the UK, this being in May 1988. Trains to/from Torness could travel via the ECML to Newcastle and then via Hexham to Carlisle but the top end of the ECML is not passed for nuclear traffic. The normal route is through the suburbs of Edinburgh to Carstairs and along the WCML.

Right: 20901+20903 at Shieldmuir on 29th May 2002 with the 6M22 Hunterston to Kingmoor flasks.

Left: This is the delightful Arten Gill Viaduct on 27th June 1999 with 20904+20906 heading towards Blea Moor with 6P99, a driver training run out and back from Kingmoor via Preston and Blackburn. Coming in at 220 yards long, the impressive viaduct stands at a height of 117 feet, carrying the railway on eleven arches.

The final part of the Class 20/9 section features the one-off one-time-only allocation of 20/9s to Hull Docks. This was 14th May 2001 when 20906+20904 powered the 6Z49 empty flats from Kingmoor to Hull. Here the train loaded up and returned to Kingmoor. As well as being the only appearance for Class 20/9s, this was actually the first train on the first day, duly making it the first time any DRS loco had worked to here. The photo left shows the train being prepared in Kingmoor. Above, the loaded train ready for the journey back.

CLASS 37

Class 37 Locomotives: 1997 to 2006				
Number	**BR Number**	**Purchased**	**Purchased From**	**DRS Livery**
37029		02/02	Riviera Trains	04/02
37038		04/03	Ian Riley	05/03
37059		09/01	EWS	01/03
37069		09/01	EWS	08/03
37087		09/04	HNRC	03/05
37194		09/04	HNRC	01/05
37197		01/06	WCRC	03/06
37218		09/01	EWS	08/02
37229		11/01	EWS	09/02
37259		02/02	Advenza/Cotswold	07/02
37261		10/05	WCRC	10/05
37510		07/05	HNRC	09/05
37515		09/04	HNRC	05/05
37602	(37502)	04/02	Eurostar	06/02
37605	(37507)	04/02	Eurostar	06/02
37606	(37508)	04/02	Eurostar	06/02
37607	(37511)	07/97	Eurostar	03/98
37608	(37512)	07/97	Eurostar	03/98
37609	(37514)	07/97	Eurostar	02/98
37610	(37687)	07/97	Eurostar	02/98
37611	(37690)	07/97	Eurostar	03/98
37612	(37691)	07/97	Eurostar	02/98
37667		09/05	HNRC	12/06
37688		09/05	EWS	10/06

The 37/6s had been renumbered prior to purchase. The previous 37/5 numbers are included for the sake of completeness. Abbreviations used: EWS = English, Welsh and Scottish Railway; HNRC = Harry Needle Railroad Company; WCRC = West Coast Railway Company.

Locomotives Named
37610 'The Malcolm Group' - Grangemouth, 14th May 2002
37229 'Jonty Jarvis 8-12-1998 to 18-3-2005' - Kingmoor, 2nd October 2005

Page 31: The Nightstar project was a costly and embarrassing blot on the history of British Railways. I principle, through trains from major UK cities to Europe sounds fine but the massive cost of implementing th required security measures along with so many other factors in running just one overnight train was staggering No disrespect intended, but on a wet Wednesday in January, how many residents of Swansea or Plymout would be desirous of an overnight train to Dortmund? Perhaps improved local train services, a late bus bac from the pub or a few more taxis on the streets would be more useful! Had these trains ever started running the locomotives opposite, complete with their ex-Mark 3 generating coach, would have been growling their wa to and from Plymouth and Swansea each night. The abandonment of this ill conceived idea wasn't so bad i the end as the purchase of all twelve locomotives certainly took the DRS story in a different direction. For th record, this is 37609+37612 running as a complete unit on a rare test run on the WCML, pictured at Carlisl in 1997.

Right: The first locomotives acquired in July 1997 arrived with DRS in their full Eurostar guise, complete with Channel Tunnel 'hole' logos. 37612+37611 were collected from the EPS depot at North Pole and ran light to Sellafield on 27th June 1997 (before the actual purchase date!). 37610+37609 were next and 37608+37607 came third. All six locos were duly branded with the DRS logo and for the first time the company had locomotives capable of 90mph. This image shows a graffiti splattered 37608 at Doncaster Works in September 1997.

Left: Hiding in the tall weeds at Hellifield, 37610+37609 head for Carlisle, running light from Doncaster during August 1997. The locos had been to this location for minor work. It must be remembered that at this time DRS only had the basic setup at Sellafield and were without the extensive facilities available at Kingmoor today.

The locos only ran in this EPS/DRS livery variation for literally a few months but they clocked up some interesting workings. Having pairs of extremely useful 37s available provided some immediate cash return with a hire to Freightliner to power their container trains. This is Southampton Maritime with 37610+37612 loading up a train for Ripple Lane. Looking at the cab end detail, in addition to all the extra cables fitted for working with a generator, they retained their blue star multiple working which meant they could work together (as seen here) and also with the 20/9s but not with the 20/3s. In later years the cab ends were stripped clean and the standard DRS multi-system was fitted.

A delightful shot of 37610 at Barrow Ramsden dock awaiting the loading of a flask from the adjacent Pacific Sandpiper. This is the same flow as pictured on page 14. The ship itself was launched in 1985 and is owned by Pacific Nuclear Transport Limited (PNTL). It is one of five such vessels operated by the company, used for the conveyance of various nuclear fuels between Japan and Europe.

DRS won a short-term contract to supply locomotives in connection with the laying of concrete troughing for signalling and cables in the Manchester area.

Looking rather work stained, and with its repaint into house colours looming, 37607 is captured at Ditton on a bleak day in January 1998.

It must be recorded that Class 20s were used mostly on the bizarre milk-less Milk Train trials of July 1997 but towards the end Class 37s were given a workout.

This is the up loop at Weaver Junction with 37609+37610. Note the lead loco is without a headboard.

From the drab EPS livery, the six 37/6s owned by DRS gained particular notoriety early in 1998 when they all received house colours. Locos 607, 608, 611 and 612 were painted at Loughborough with 609 and 610 being treated at Doncaster.

37609 was first out, seen here at Kirkconnel Station with a Doncaster to Kilmarnock road learning trip in February 1998. With its white tyres and spotless yellow ends, the loco looks a million dollars.

On 6th April 2000, 37607+37609 were running light engine from Kingmoor to Falkland Yard at Ayr when they were requisitioned to rescue a failed Class 87 powering 1M08, the 06.15 from Glasgow to London Euston. With the train at a standstill at Wamphray (between Beattock and Lockerbie) the 37s took charge and worked through to Carlisle. Although only about 35 miles in distance, this was quite a notable working, and reaching a credible 90mph en-route this was one of the better Virgin Trains rescues of modern times! Compare this image of 37609 to the previous one from a year earlier. Note the significant alterations to the cab end detail with the group standard head/tail light cluster, roof mounted additional headlight and DRS multi-working system socket.

On 15th May 1999 a pair of DRS Class 37/6s were requested for Eagle Railtours 'The North York Moors Explorer' and 37611 and 37612 were selected. This remarkable photograph on the tight curve at St. Andrews Junction, Birmingham, shows what was the empty stock on its way from Carnforth to Worcester (via Tyseley) the day before. 20313+20314 had hitched a lift south to work another Eagle Railtours train on the Sunday. Running as 'The Cambrian Mountain Explorer' the 20s worked from Birmingham New Street to Aberystwyth and back. The main tour on the Saturday saw 37611+37612 work the train from Worcester Shrub Hill to Birmingham New Street thcn Derby, Chesterfield, Doncaster, York, Eaglescliffe and Middlesbrough finally terminating at Battersby. From here, the BR green liveried 47488 took the train forward to Whitby. After a three hour layover, the same 47 worked back to Battersby and the 37s powered the train back to Worcester via a similar route to the outward journey.

Below: Another unexpected flow for which DRS gained a contract was the running of coal trains between Ayr and Carlisle Yard. It came about when EWS suffered a shortage of both locomotives and crews and pairs of 37/6s were used on two trains in each direction on weekdays. The trains of loaded coal were worked from Ayr to Carlisle Yard by the 37s. Here they were swapped for a Class 66 and the train continued to Fiddlers Ferry, Drax or other power stations as required. In turn, a Class 66 (or perhaps a 56 or even 2 x 37) brought in the empties and the DRS 37/6s headed to Scotland. The job lasted for about nine months during 2000 and it gave the opportunity to see, film and photograph Type 3s working lengthy trains of HAA hoppers over the scenic GSW route. This stunning image shows 37608+37609 on the Up Goods Flyover about to enter the yard at Carlisle.

Right: Can you hear it? On 6th June 2000, 37609+37607 shatter the silence at the picturesque location of Enterkinfoot, near Drumlanrig Tunnel with the 6M04, the 14.30 Ayr to Carlisle. This particular train had consisted of 1766 tonnes of coal!

Left: A third shot of the coal trains shows 37612+37610 at Closeburn. Six years before this image was taken, back in 1994, 37694 (610) was working off Immingham in the two tone grey Railfreight livery with Construction branding whilst 37691 (612) was also at Immingham, wearing the Railfreight red stripe livery! Both locos would have worked this type of train on a regular basis.

Right: Another trial service that DRS ran involved Carlisle based road haulier Eddie Stobart for five days in 1998. As the story goes, it was to see how (empty) bottled products travelled by rail in a curtain-sided vehicle. Basically, would any smash! The train itself ran a fair old journey from Daventry to Hunterston and back and the Stobart branded wagon can clearly be seen in this delightful shot on the Clydeport Causeway with 37612+37608 in charge. It was not established if any bottles did break but the trial was deemed unsuccessful and no further trains ran. Eight years later in 2006, DRS, Eddie Stobart and Tesco joined forces to bring us the 'Tesco Express' and this train will feature in the second volume in this series.

On 12th March 2003 speed trials were undertaken to see how loaded and unloaded FNA wagons coped with speeds of 45 and 60mph. With 37608 in charge, the two flasks were joined by the Serco Railtest former Mark 2 FK coach 975290 and ran from Derby to Carnforth and back. Pictured at Carnforth, the consist is about to return south.

Left: Not content with their own six 37/6s, from time to time DRS hired in some of the other EPS owned locomotives and for a while during 1999, 37604 moved north. In no time at all the loco was in regular use and this delightful image shows it passing through Arnside station with 20308 and the 6K73 flasks from Sellafield to Crewe. As well as being the wrong way around as such, these locos could not work in multiple. 37604 would eventually join the DRS ranks for real in 2008.

Top right: April 2002 saw the purchase of three more Class 37/6s, 602, 605 and 606. This left Eurostar with just the three, 37601, 37603 and 37604. Pictured at Kingmoor in July of that year, 37602 arrived with all the additional front end cables and equipment intact. Not long after this picture was taken, 37602 along with 605 and 606 were moved to Glasgow Works for repaints.

Bottom right: This remarkable picture shows 37602 at Springburn station on 23rd May 2002 during its repaint! With patches of body filler and a hole cut next to the headlight for the multiple working socket, this was an incredible working to say the least. As the story goes, during the repaint it was necessary to turn the locomotive so it was sent on its own – minus any bodyside numbers or branding – from the works into Springburn station, reverse, to Motherwell, reverse, to Mossend East Junction, reverse, back to Springburn and into the Works complex.

July 2002 and the completed 37602 at Glasgow Works awaiting collection and movement to Carlisle. As these two images show, 37606 was also repainted at this time alongside 33030, the second Class 33 to receive house colours. Looking at both 37s and although they have retained the now obsolete jumper and multi-working cables for hauling the Nightstar stock, note that both have had a small hole cut next to the headlight which has subsequently been sealed up. This was later used for the DRS multi-working sockets as the next page reveals.

Top right: The once cable-cluttered front ends of the 37/6s changed completely in 2002/2003 with this rather bland and faceless look. Removing all cables from the cab ends, including the blue star multiple working and plating over any former headcode boxes or marker lights, this new rather bland look for the Class 37 was not very well received by enthusiasts. For the company, the fitting of their in-house multiple working sockets meant that for the first time these locos could work with the 20/3s and the group standard marker/head/tail light clusters with a roof mounted additional headlight brought the locomotives right up date with current legislation. This image shows 37605 with 20315 and 37602 at the north end of the LNWR depot at Crewe in August 2004.

Bottom right: 37607 freshly painted in what was its second coat of DRS blue in February 2003 with 47237 at the Brush site at Loughborough.

Around about the time the second batch of 37/6s arrived DRS set about gathering up numerous 37/0s and 37/3s with the intention of restoring some to mainline status. At this point the company had only bought the 'as new' 37/6s so any subsequent purchases were going to involve full overhauls or least some work to get them roadworthy again. Similar to the Class 20s, the company bought just about every available loco they could and sent many of them to the Brush complex at Loughborough. Some of the locomotives had already been for component recovery at Wigan and arrived bogie-less, engine-less and one step shy of being scrapped. These two images show some of the locos at Brush in early 2002 with your classic nose end depot-shot line up. All is not what it seems as all the locos here are on temporary rails and the sun bleached liveries tell a tale of years of open storage. Of the two nearest the camera, 37262 the former Inverness based 'Dounreay', was active until the end of 1999 and was probably in a reasonable condition. This loco was not selected and was scrapped in February 2004. 37340 (below) also missed the cut but made it into preservation and, at the time of writing, is undergoing restoration at the Great Central Railway in its earlier guise of D6709/37009.

37229 was one of the 37/0s purchased from EWS which made it back to main line status, as these images show. Wearing a tired coat of the two tone grey Railfreight livery with Coal sector branding, the loco was withdrawn from service at the end of the 1999 leaf fall/sandite season and stored at Cardiff. Formerly named 'The Cardiff Road Mill' the loco was subsequently towed to Kingmoor where it is pictured in front of an ex-works 33030 in July 2002. Unlike many other 37s this loco did not receive any modifications to its front end during overhaul, retaining the blue star system. The DRS multi-working socket hole was cut and panelled over and as of 2011, had yet to be fitted! The loco was named 'Jonty Jarvis 8-12-1998 to 18-3-2005' at Carlisle in October 2005. Note the dusty bogies in the ex-works shot at Glasgow from October 2002.

Having selected various withdrawn 37/0s for overhaul, a further batch of locomotives were acquired from other operators. As the table on page 30 shows, companies such as HNRC had also purchased withdrawn locos from EWS and returned them to mainline status. One of the more interesting purchases involved 37029. This loco had a fairly uneventful existence until it was withdrawn in December 1993. Purchased by Pete Waterman in March 1994 the loco was initially used on numerous preserved lines and made it back to the mainline in 1998. Displayed at the Warley Model Railway Exhibition in October 1999, the loco was sold to Riviera Trains which saw it paired up with 37038 to work various rugby specials to Cardiff in 2000/2001. DRS acquired the locomotive in February 2002 and as it was serviceable and mainline registered, it was quickly painted and put to use. The photo on the left shows the loco in down recess sidings at Lockerbie, being towed by 37609 in April 2002. Note the reinstated and working headcode boxes! Unfortunately, the headcode boxes were filled in with yellow plastic complete with two cut out circles per box as can be seen! The photo to the right shows the loco at Park Sidings at Plymouth on 23rd May 2006 with a road learning trip.

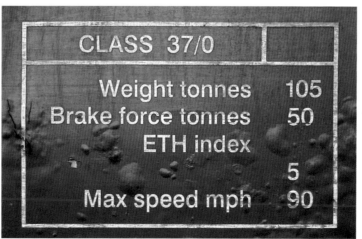

CLASS 37/0	
Weight tonnes	105
Brake force tonnes	50
ETH index	5
Max speed mph	90

DRS

Direct Rail Services

The third 37/0 to come into traffic for DRS in 2002 was 37259. This was another former EWS machine, sold to Cotswold Rail in August 2001 and sent to Loughborough for overhaul. At this time the loco was numbered 37380 and was running on a set of re-geared CP7 bogies (and classified as a 37/3). During the overhaul DRS purchased the locomotive, it received a normal set of bogies and duly emerged as 37259 (and was re-classified back to 37/0 status). This interesting photo at the works from 2003 shows the partial front end blank-out. This was a busy period for the works with classes 33, 37 and 47 all undergoing attention. Behind 37259 here is 47206 which was converted to 57605 for Great Western sleeper trains and behind that, 37211, another DRS loco but one which never made into service.

Left: Looking at this image, you wouldn't think this loco was salvaged from the scrap man and returned to such a wonderful condition. This is 37069, one of the numerous EWS locomotives which worked in France in 1999/2000. Upon return to England, it was almost immediately sent to Wigan for component recovery and parts were removed before DRS purchased the loco in September 2001. After an overhaul at Loughborough in 2002/2003, which included the blank front end look and DRS multi-working socket, but not the removal of the vacuum brakes, 37069 was one of three more 37/0s in traffic by summer 2003. 37038 and 37059 were the other two.

Right: 37194 was one of the locomotives purchased from HNRC and was repainted in DRS colours at Barrow Hill. Of all the 37/0s which DRS have operated so far this loco is probably the most unmodified as this lovely image proves. Retaining vacuum brakes, snowploughs and even the blue star symbols, 37194 is paired with 37029 at Greenfield Junction, Gateshead whilst working 6E44, the 07.43 Carlisle to Seaton-on-Tees flasks on 17th June 2006.

Left: 37087 spent most of its life in Eastern England, working off Gateshead, Thornaby, Stratford and March depots. Between 1976 and 1989 it was a regular on passenger and freight duties in East Anglia. With its steam heat boiler it would have worked expresses out of Liverpool Street to the likes of Cambridge, Kings Lynn and Norwich for many years. In the early/mid 1990s the loco moved to Scotland, working passenger, freight and sleeper services whilst based at Eastfield, Inverness and Motherwell. Unofficially named 'Vulcan' for many years, the name became official (as 'VULCAN AVRO B1 & B2') in 2003 whilst under the ownership of HNRC. Sold to DRS in September 2004 in full working order, the loco retained its split headcode boxes and many other original features as seen here at Currock Junction on 7th August 2006 with 37038 working the 6M60 return flasks from Seaton to Carlisle.

Top right: With various 37/0s and 37/6s on board the next part of the DRS story involved the purchase and return to service of four 37/5s. This sub class will be dealt with in more detail in the second book but for the sake of completeness, the four locos returned to service were 37510 and 37515 in 2005 and 37667 and 37688 in 2006. The photo opposite shows 37510 at Urlay Nook working the 4Z44 Kingmoor to Haverton Hill flats on 4th April 2007.

Bottom right: 37688, with the name 'KINGMOOR TMD' (named 7th July 2007) is seen at Faulkland Junction working another train of flats coming off repair at Kilmarnock and heading for Kingmoor. The date here is 14th April 2009.

CLASS 33

Class 33 Locomotives: 2000 to 2005				
Number	Purchased	Purchased From	DRS Livery	Sold
33025	11/01	EWS	06/02	09/05
33029	12/00	HNRC	03/05	09/05
33030	11/01	EWS	05/02	09/05
33207	12/00	HNRC	05/01	09/05

All four locomotives were sold to the West Coast Railway Company. Abbreviations used: EWS = English, Welsh and Scottish Railway; HNRC = Harry Needle Railroad Company.

Looking back now, the purchase and subsequent operation of Class 33s may well beg the question why? The answer is probably not too dissimilar from why the Class 20s were bought back on day one, they were available at a good price and suited traffic requirements perfectly at the time. With the Class 66 dominant, EWS decided to keep some of their better locomotives, namely classes 37 and 47 for a while longer, while classes such as 31 and 33 were withdrawn, and scrapped or sold off fairly quickly. A number of Class 33s were purchased at the end of 2000 including 33008, the former 'Eastleigh' celebrity. In the end, as we now know, only four ever made it into service with the company and by September 2005 it was all over.

Page 57 top: This first photograph was, at the time, nothing to do with the DRS Class 33 fleet and was simply a job which the company been asked to do. Running as 0F81 on 20th August 1999, 20309+20305 hauled 47701 and 33207 from Tyseley to Derby RTC. 47701, owned by Fragonset at the time, had suffered a bogie fire at Birmingham New Street three months earlier and 33207, owned by HNRC, was en-route to Derby for overhaul. The train is pictured upon arrival at Derby.

Page 57 bottom: Looks can be deceiving, or are they? This is Kingmoor depot in December 2000 shortly after the delivery of 33029 and 33023. If you had to pick the best one, start it up and run it around the yard, perhaps you'd go with 33023. Wrong! This loco was indeed started up and moved around the yard and was subsequently transferred to Glasgow Works (see page 46) but not to be overhauled. As it turned out, it was discovered to have a bent underframe so was used to provide spares for 33025 and 33030 and was scrapped in 2005. With the demise of this loco, DRS chose the rather beaten and weather-worn 33029 but this didn't go to plan either. Moved to the FM Rail workshops in Derby, the overhaul took a staggering four years and it wasn't until April 2005 before the locomotive was back at Kingmoor in a coat of DRS blue.

Left: 33207 became the first Class 33 locomotive to work for DRS when, upon completion of the overhaul and repaint at the Fragonset Works in Derby, it was dispatched to Kingmoor in May 2001. As the photo and text on the previous page explains, this loco was to be overhauled for HNRC but during the work it was sold to DRS. Looking exceptionally smart in house colours the loco is pictured at Loughbrough in 2003.

Right: A delightful shot at Kingmoor of 33025 and 33030 with 37610 from July 2002. Fitted with snowploughs (even in July!) the two 33s were overhauled and painted in the DRS livery at Glasgow Works. They arrived at Kingmoor on 9th July and 14th June 2002 respectively.

Left: The locos were never fitted with the DRS multi-working system, retaining their blue star method which, other than the 20/3s and modified 37s, meant they could work with other members of the fleet. Although often paired, one such mixed 33/37 working was recorded on 19th July 2002 when 33025+37602 worked the Kingmoor – Hunterston flask train. Pictured at Hunterston High Level, the locos are pictured heading back to England. To the right is the coal loading facility. Imported coal brought in by ship is carried along the conveyor belt (to the left) and then dropped into coal hoppers between the two towers. This turned out to be an interesting day for 33025!

The only occasion when a DRS Class 33 worked a passenger train was on 19th July 2002 when 33025 was sent to rescue a failed 87002 at Eden Valley, just south of Penrith. As it turned out, 33025+37602 had just arrived back from Hunterston (from previous page) and were on Kingmoor depot when an emergency call came in, saying that the 87 was a complete failure. It was even unable to roll down the hill to Carlisle! The 33 was uncoupled from the 37 and dispatched light engine to Penrith where it crossed over and came across the failed train. Working the 24 mile journey to Carlisle, it is understood Virgin Trains control wanted the 33 to carry on to Glasgow but a combination of insufficient fuel and driver hours saw the 33 detached and sent back light to Kingmoor. However, for some 20-odd minutes after arrival at Carlisle, the 33 remained atop and nearly made a significant piece of railway history. The top photo shows the scene at Eden Valley prior to departure. The bottom photo shows the train upon arrival at Carlisle. For the record, the working was 1S75, the 12.25 Euston to Glasgow.

Sixty-one pages in and yet another freight flow which was trialled with DRS! On the back of (empty) milk trains and (empty) bottle trains came Minimodal! The idea was simply a smaller version of the intermodal traffic wagons with six smaller containers on the one modified megafret rather than just one large one. In principle the logic was there and the idea was to appeal to small businesses who did not want or could not afford larger containers but still wanted the 'greener' rail option. On 11th September 2002 a demonstration train operated from Kingmoor to the NRM at York using the 'Minimodal' branded 33025+33030 in top and tail mode. The top photo shows the demonstration train on Kingmoor prior to departure with 33030 as the lead loco. 33025 is pictured at Glasgow Works on 9th July 2002. Guess what happened next? Nothing!

It was decided to include this lovely image of 33025, a filthy dirty 20312 and a couple of flats in between them on Kingmoor depot. No further details came with this slide so it's guesswork but with a tail lamp on the back of the 33, was this train about to depart with the 20 leading and running nose first?

The DRS Class 33 story ended on 15th September 2005 when the four locomotives were transferred to Carnforth, coming under the ownership and operation of the West Coast Railway Company. Although extremely useful, with their 60mph top speed (reduced from 85mph) and ETS supply, they were not much good to DRS whereas WCRC had significant passenger work, all of which required locos with an ETS supply and lesser duties on the Royal Scotsman. By this time 33030 had suffered traction motor problems and then an engine failure but 33029 was almost in mint condition. The deal between the two companies involved the four 33s to WCRC and in return for them, two fully serviceable Class 37s in the shape of 37197 and 37261. It's not known if it was a straight swap or if cash, parts, labour or repainting was part of the deal. The WCRC lost two great locos, DRS added two perfectly compatible 37/0s to their ever expanding fleet and both were painted in DRS colours at Carnforth. These two photographs show the final train from Kingmoor, on what was a very wet day. Note that 33030 had lost its 'Minimodal' branding whilst 33025 still retained it and the 'BI' headcode on the back. The four loco convoy was then pictured at Kitchen Hill, just north of Penrith in torrential rain.

CLASS 47

Class 47 Locomotives: 2002 to 2006				
Number	Purchased	Purchased From	DRS Livery	Sold/Scrapped
47237	09/02	EWS	02/03	Sold 12/07 to Cotswold Rail
47298	09/02	EWS	04/03	Withdrawn 10/6. Scrapped 05/07
47501	05/02	Brailsford Engineering	07/03	
47802	05/02	Alstom Traincare	11/02	
Abbreviations used: EWS = English, Welsh and Scottish Railway				

In a similar vein to the three Classes already featured, DRS purchased various Class 47s over the years and this book features the first four that were restored to traffic. It must have been seriously questioned as to why a freight operating company, principally involved with the movement of low-key short trains over equally short distances at speeds not exceeding 60mph would want with a huge Type 4 locomotive, designed for heavy freight and express passenger and mail trains. The answer to this became clear in later years but right from the early days the company clearly had more ambitious plans than just hauling single flask trains and the 47s in particular the 47/4s, helped realise this ambition. It was May 2002 when the 47501 and 47802 were purchased. 47501 had spent many years in South Wales and the west, working off Cardiff, Laira, Landore and Old Oak Common and it was named 'Craftsman' in 1987. By spring of 1999 it was all over and the loco was destined to go to Wigan for component recovery. The move never took place and it was sold to Brailsford Engineering with the idea of operating the loco under the Fragonset banner. Nothing came of this until May 2002 when it was resold to DRS and by autumn 2002 it was at Glasgow Works undergoing an overhaul. In the end it took the best part of nine months to complete the overhaul and it was late summer 2003 before the locomotive was working off Kingmoor. At the same time in 2002, DRS acquired 47802. This loco was numerically the second 47/4 to be converted for the famous Inter City Cross-Country ILRA pool, this in 1989 and it included the long range fuel tanks. When was realised Inter City didn't need 53 such locomotives, many were converted to Rail Express Systems 47/7s but for 47802 in particular, it was dropped by Inter City and not wanted by RES either so it spent much of its time on low key engineers trains and obscure unit moves. Destined for a one way trip to Wigan, the loco was purchased by Alstom with the intention of using it on unit moves between their plant at Washwood Heath in Birmingham and the various TMDs around the UK. Admitted to Glasgow Works for overhaul in November 2001, it is understood Alstom 'changed their minds' and with work having already started, it was cancelled but DRS were quick off the mark and purchased the loco. In November 2002, 47802 became the first operational DRS Class 47. Somewhat ironically, at the time of writing, 47802s future looks secure whereas many of the 47/4s renumbered/converted to the 47/8 series have now been scrapped or are stored/withdrawn.

Page 65: 47237 is pictured at Loughborough in 2003. This loco was acquired in September 2002 and was moved to Glasgow Works for overhaul. Upon completion it received the in-house multi-working sockets which enabled it to work in multiple with the 20/3s and like-fitted 37s. This gave the possibility of a 47 working in multiple with a Class 20, something that never happened in BR days and even the pairing of Sulzer/English Electric locos sounds weird! Unfortunately, as far as the DRS story goes, although it was often described as a great locomotive by drivers, a change in company policy in favour of ETS fitted 47s saw this loco sold to Cotswold Rail/Advenza at the end of 2007. Following the demise of this company and a lengthy period of storage at Gloucester, it was purchased by WCRC in early 2011 and a move back north was expected.

Left: Opened by British Rail in 1968, closed in 1988, then reopened by DRS in 1998, today Kingmoor depot can undertake a significant amount of work. As well as the wash and fuel facilities, here in the main shed a variety of jobs can be carried out including complete engine changes, body repairs, bogie swaps and traction motor swaps. The only major facility missing is a dedicated Paint Shop! This lovely depot shot at Kingmoor from 31st October 2004 shows 47237, 47298 and 66401. Note how clean and tidy the workshop looks.

Right: The image shows 47501 on Matterson 35 tonne jacks. The 4 x 35 tonne jacks mean you can lift 140 tonnes if it is evenly distributed and with your 47/4 coming in at about 125 tonnes, including bogies, this is a quite a manageable lift. 1st May 2007.

Right: This is Norwood Junction, Gateshead on 4th June 2007 with 47237 on its way back with the repaired flats from Haverton Hill.

Left: It may be a misconceived perception looking back now, but for many years after their entry into service the 47s seemed to spend most of their days on Kingmoor. Researching such workings drew many blanks and the locos appear to have been disused for weeks at a time. Quite often they worked short trips to Sellafield and back and these were rarely photographed or recorded. Often during the hours of darkness, a spare loco off Kingmoor would run light to Sellafield and return with a single wagon or empty flat. These journeys were often done to maintain driver knowledge on the 47s or just to keep them operational. The overnight Malcolm trains between Daventry and Grangemouth employed 47s from time to time but again, in winter, both journeys were under darkness. One of the trains that seemed to attract the odd 2 x 47 was the Hartlepool flasks. On 3rd May 2006, 47298+47802 did the honours, seen here at King Edward Bridge Junction, Gateshead with the 6M60 return train.

Two images of 47802+47298 with two very different trainloads. Top, this is Logan's Road crossing, just north of Motherwell on 2nd May 2006 and 6M22 from Hunterston to Kingmoor. 47298 only worked for DRS for a short while. Being withdrawn by EWS in January 1999 it was acquired in September 2002 and returned to operational status in May 2003 after receiving an overhaul and repaint at Glasgow Works. After just four years of sporadic working, the loco suffered a serious generator fault whilst climbing Beattock in October 2006. The damage was deemed too expensive to repair and with the policy shift to purchasing ETS-fitted locos, the end had come. Ironically, twelve months after this picture was taken, the loco was broken for scrap at Booths in Rotherham. The loco has a double claim-to-fame. Firstly, the positioning of its fleet numbers, which were higher than all the rest. This was done to enable a customer logo to be affixed underneath but it never came to fruition. Secondly, although DRS bought many locomotives over the years and then re-sold/scrapped them, 47298 is, as it stands, the only one to be fully restored and duly withdrawn and scrapped. The second image shows the same pair of locos at Blea Moor signal box on 22nd April 2006 whilst working a loaded train of Railtrack liveried ballast hoppers from Carlisle Yard to Basford Hall (on behalf of Freightliner). Coming in at 1128 tonnes, this gave the 47s a bit more to think about, but they did what they had to do!

Top: After the initial batch of 47s, things were quiet for many years and by 2010, the company had purchased some more, including both early and late versions of the 47/7, mainly from the demise of other companies. These will be dealt with in the second volume but for the sake of completeness, as at the end of 2010, 47712, 47790, 47810, 47832 and 47841 were all operational. In May 2007 the first boost to the DRS owned 47 fleet was the purchase of the two former 'Blue Pullman' 47/7s, 709 and 712. Previously owned and operated by FM Rail, these much travelled and multi-liveried locomotives had become available following the demise of the company in 2006. Painted in the nanking blue livery and named 'Dionysos' and 'Artemis' respectively, the duo were pictured at Kingmoor on 3rd June 2007.

Bottom: One final piece of the story worth recording was the short term lease and subsequent minimal use of a number of Riviera Trains owned 47/4s in 2006. In a complicated and twisted saga, DRS were, apparently 'short of locomotives' and asked their Crewe based colleagues for help. By October 2006, eight locomotives were in the XHNC pool, based at Kingmoor. By November the same eight were back at Crewe in the Riviera Trains RTLO pool! For the record, the eight locos were 47805, 47812, 47815, 47839, 47843, 47847, 47848 and 47853. This image shows one of them, 47805 'Talisman', at Kingmoor in October 2006.

OTHER CLASSES

Class 08 Locomotives: 2006 to 2009				
Number	**Purchased**	**Purchased From**	**DRS Livery**	**Sold**
08834	05/06	RFS Doncaster	08/06	01/09
08892	05/06	RFS Doncaster	07/06	01/09
Both locos were sold to the Harry Needle Railroad Company.				

Page 71: Two further short lived and little used purchases were of 08834 and 08892. The original plan was to use one of them on the aforementioned Sellafield to Drigg run with the other either spare or hired out. Painted in July (08892) and August (08834) of 2006 at Doncaster, due to the shape of the bonnet the full logo couldn't be applied so the D R S letters were placed individually along the bonnet and the DIRECT RAIL SERVICES sticker on the fuel tank. Looking very smart indeed the locos are pictured at Kingmoor on 20th October 2006. After being leased to various companies they were both sold outright to HNRC in January 2009.

Class 87 Locomotives: 2004 to 2005				
Number	**Leased**	**Leased From**	**DRS Livery**	**Lease Ended**
87006	09/04	Porterbrook	12/04	07/05
87022	09/04	Porterbrook	11/04	07/05
87028	09/04	Porterbrook	12/04	06/05

Page 72: In 2004 yet another trial with another class of locomotive took place and this time it was the Class 87. Built specifically with WCML duties in mind, could these ex-Virgin Trains provide an alternative to diesel power for DRS? The answer, rather unfortunately was no, but for a short period in 2004-2005, Class 87s were back on freight duties.

To prove how serious DRS were about the 87s, the three locomotives they acquired were painted into the house colours. 87022, the former 'The Black Prince' lost its Virgin colours at Crewe in November 2004 and this was followed by 87006 ('George Reynolds') and 87028 ('Lord President') in December. These two images capture a remarkable series of events that took place late on New Year's Eve 2004 when the two 87s arrived at Carlisle station freshly painted from Crewe and were taken the last few miles to Kingmoor by 37612+37602.

Top: As recorded in the previous caption, 87022 was painted in November 2004 and is pictured here on the 20th on the wall siding at Carlisle in between driver training duties.

Bottom: There were a number of reasons why DRS terminated the lease of these locomotives and one of the key factors was their use on the Daventry – Grangemouth Intermodals. Running under the wires all the way from Daventry to Mossend wasn't a problem and the locos coped considerably better with Shap and Beattock than a Class 66 (or any diesel) ever would. At Mossend, a loco change was required and as well as adding time to the journey, it wasn't possible to stable a loco or perform such a task in the EWS owned yard. The 87s could have continued further down the line to Coatbridge, but this facility is owned and operated by Freightliner. Problems also arose with getting the 87s on, off and maintaining them at the non-electrified Kingmoor depot. In the end the locos were out of use by April 2005 and went off lease soon after. Today, amazingly, they are still painted in the DRS colours hauling trains in Bulgaria! This photo shows 87022 atop 66407 at Carlisle Upperby on a driver training run on 30th November 2004 with 4M44 to Daventry. *(Keith Hayton x 4)*

Top left: With rival freight companies EWS, Freightliner and GBRf acquiring Class 66 locomotives in the 1998-2002 period it only seemed a natural progression that DRS would follow suit. Having trialled the GBRf owned 66/7s on the overnight Malcolm trains in 2002/2003, an order was placed for ten Class 66s. Initially suggested they would be numbered as 66801 upwards and delivered to Workington Docks, it was 16th October 2003 when the M V Fairlift docked at Newport and on board were 66401 to 405. On 18th November 2003, the same ship brought in 66406 to 66410 and the DRS Class 66 story was underway. Initially trialled and tested on a variety of duties from water cannon trains to single flask trains with a loco on each end, the locos gained more notoriety working Intermodals on the WCML and 66405 was branded for 'W H Malcolm'. It is often presumed that DRS own these locos but in fact they are owned by Halifax Assets Finance Ltd. and leased to the company. Bath time for 66401 at Kingmoor on 7th June 2006.

Bottom left: The third batch of Class 66s arrived in the UK on 29th May 2006 and this included 66411 to 66413. Fresh off the ship, 66411 stands at the dockside awaiting a move to Kingmoor. This particular locomotive gained worldwide press coverage just a few months later when 'Eddie the Engine' and the Tesco train was born but that's another story for another day.

Page 75: In total 34 Class 66/4s have operated for DRS to date with the last four, 66431 to 66434 arriving in November 2008. Before these locos had even turned a wheel, a decision was made to take the first ten locos off lease and in October/November 2008, 66401 to 66410 were stored. This image goes back to 9th September 2007 with the 'M V Fairpartner' at Newport and left to right at the back are 66426, 66424 and 66425 with, front row left to right, 66422, 66421, 66427 and 66423.

Page 76: The decision by Freightliner to dispense with the services of their twelve 57/0 locomotives in 2007 opened up a new opportunity for DRS and by 2010 nine were leased by the company. Owned by Porterbrook, the availability of these machines may well have influenced the decision to send the first ten Class 66/4s off lease in 2008. All of them were subsequently fitted with the DRS multi-working system. Pictured inside the main shed at Kingmoor, 57003 is raised off its bogies receiving attention on 2nd August 2008. Previously named 'Freightliner Evolution' this is the former 47317, previously named 'Willesden Yard'.

Top right: An early shot of 57012 and 57008 at Kingmoor from 24th May 2007. Note that both locos were leased to DRS with their names of 'Freightliner Envoy' and 'Freightliner Explorer'. This is quite unusual as it is often common practice for the outgoing TOC to remove such personal items and either sell or reuse them.

Bottom right: All nine of the DRS 57/0s have been outshopped in the new 'Compass' livery and it suits the flush body of the 47s and 57s quite well. Centre road at Carlisle on 20th May 2008 with 57012 and an exceptionally short rake of two flats. 57011 was actually the first of the 57s to be seen in the new livery, being unveiled at the Kingmoor open day in July 2007.

The final selection of images show Carlisle Kingmoor depot over the years. Anybody with a spotting book from the 1970s or 1980s would have known this depot as KD (not the KM which it is today) and selecting a year at random, 1986, 25 years ago at the time of writing, it was home to various Class 08, 25, 31 and 47 locomotives plus the sole surviving Class 40, 40122 (D200). The depot closed in 1988 and these images show it in early 1998, shortly before DRS took over. Top left is the main shed as seen on page 59. Bottom left is looking north with the fuel plant visible and bottom right is looking south towards Carlisle station itself with the wash plant in view. Considering it had been ten years since closure, the site does not appear to have suffered any serious vandalism and the weeds had yet to take a serious hold.

Top: So far there have been four successful open days at Kingmoor, taking place in 2003, 2005, 2007 and 2009 and a fifth is planned for 2011. This image comes from the first one in 2003 with four of the five classes of locomotive which the company owned at the time lined up for visitors to see.

Bottom: Without meaning to sound disrespectful in any way, when DRS purchased their first locomotives the facilities they had with which to maintain them was little more than a couple of guys with a bag or two of spanners and a handful of spare parts! To be fair it wasn't as grim as that but in comparison, this is what they can do today, as 20303 has its engine lifted out at Kingmoor on 13th September 2008.

BACK IN ACTION: With overhauls completed, including reconditioned power units installed, Class 37/4 Nos. 37419 and 37425 are pictured at Barrow Hill awaiting their new lease of life with new owner DRS. The date was March 24. HNRC

Riding the **Workington Shuttle**

The story of the DRS operated Maryport to Workington shuttle trains including a Cab Ride from Carlisle to Workington

Produced with the full assistance of Direct Rail Services

...n't really associate DRS ...oal trains but for a while ...s were used between Ayr ...37608+37607 with a huge ...on the single line branch ...d Mauchline Junction.

...t of this book may be reproduced ...or by any means, electronic or ...ocopying, scanning, recording or by any information storage and retrieval system, without written permission from the publisher.
Published by Videoscene, PO Box 243, Lytham St. Annes. FY8 9DE